MAR 1 2 2014

Essential Life Science

LIFE PROCESSES

Louise and Richard Spilsbury

Heinemann
LIBRARY

Chicago, Illinois

Edited by Andrew Farrow and Diyan Leake
Designed by Victoria Allen
Original illustrations © Capstone Global
    Library Ltd 2014
Picture research by Ruth Blair
Production by Sophia Argyris
Originated by Capstone Global Library Ltd
Printed in China by CTPS

17 16 15 14 13
10 9 8 7 6 5 4 3 2

Library of Congress Cataloging-in-Publication Data
Spilsbury, Louise
  Life processes / Louise and Richard Spilsbury.
      pages cm.—(Essential life science)
  Includes bibliographical references and index.
  ISBN 978-1-4329-7810-5 (hardback)—ISBN 978-1-4329-7841-9 (paperback) 1. Physiology—Juvenile literature. I. Spilsbury, Richard, 1963-. II. Title.
  QP37.S728 2014
  571—dc23   2012051332

Acknowledgments
We would like to thank the following for permission to reproduce photographs: Alamy p. 14 (© Juniors Bildarchiv GmbH); Capstone Publishers (© Karon Dubke) pp. 12,13, 16, 17, 24, 25; Corbis pp. 19 (© David Spurdens/www.ExtremeSportsPhoto.com), 20 (© Heidi & Hans-Juergen Koch/Minden Pictures); Getty Images pp. 9 (Bob Elsdale), 23 (Franois De Heel), 26 (Morales), 28 (Visuals Unlimited, Inc./Ken Catania), 32 (Ed Reschke), 33 (Jeff Rotman), 34 (David Wrobel), 35 (Westend61), 37 (Tetra Images), 38 (Image by Ruben Moreno Montoliu), 39 (Photolibrary/Gary Lewis); Shutterstock pp. 6 (© siwasasil), 7 (© Marco Uliana), 11 (© zixian), 21 (© ermess), 22 (© artjazz), 29 (© Taiga), 30 (© Portokalis); Superstock pp. 4 (Gohier/VWPics), 5 (imagebroker.net), 10 (Lars Schneider/Aurora Open), 36 (imagebroker.net), 40 (NaturePL), 42 (Natalie Fobes/Science Faction), 43 (Minden Pictures).

Cover photograph of a puffin reproduced with permission of Shutterstock (© Doug Berndt).

Every effort has been made to contact copyright holders of material reproduced in this book. Any omissions will be rectified in subsequent printings if notice is given to the publisher.

Disclaimer
All the Internet addresses (URLs) given in this book were valid at the time of going to press. However, due to the dynamic nature of the Internet, some addresses may have changed, or sites may have changed or ceased to exist since publication. While the author and publisher regret any inconvenience this may cause readers, no responsibility for any such changes can be accepted by either the author or the publisher.

Contents

Eureka moment!

Learn about important discoveries that have brought about further knowledge and understanding.

DID YOU KNOW?

Discover fascinating facts about life processes.

WHAT'S NEXT?

Read about the latest research and advances in essential science.

Some words are shown in bold, **like this**. You can find out what they mean by looking in the glossary.

What Are Life Processes?

There are millions of different types of living things on Earth, from ants to zebras and from bamboo to daffodils. What they all have in common is that they carry out seven life processes. A life process is a process that allows living things to survive and maintain themselves.

The seven processes

- Movement: Moving parts of the body
- **Respiration**: Releasing energy from food
- Sensitivity: Reacting and responding to changes—for example, taking shelter from cold or other dangers
- **Nutrition**: Getting food, which is the source of energy for living things
- **Excretion**: Getting rid of waste from the body
- **Reproduction**: Creating new versions of themselves that will survive once they have died
- Growth: Getting bigger and repairing injuries.

We can remember the processes by the name made from the first letter of each word: Mrs. Nerg!

Orcas risk getting stuck on beaches when they hunt sea lions, to meet their nutritional needs.

A thing is not alive if it does not carry out all seven processes. For example, a car can move, release energy, get rid of waste, and even react to the world around it, like an animal. But no car can grow or reproduce, so it is nonliving.

Maintaining life processes

A car only works if it has fuel and its engine and wheels are maintained. Life processes can only continue if a living thing gets what it needs from the **environment**—the conditions in which it lives. Most living things need air, water, food, and space to survive.

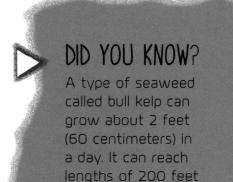

DID YOU KNOW?

A type of seaweed called bull kelp can grow about 2 feet (60 centimeters) in a day. It can reach lengths of 200 feet (65 meters).

For many animals, reproduction includes caring for their young, to make sure the young survive and may one day reproduce themselves.

How Do Living Things Feed?

Living things need food to survive. Nutrition is all about getting enough of the right type of food. Food contains substances that provide energy. It also contains other substances that are essential for growth and repair. Most animals eat food, but green plants make their own food.

Many green plants, such as these water lilies, have leaves with a wide surface area. This is to take in light that they use to make food for their nutrition.

Eureka moment!

In 1977, Colleen Cavanaugh discovered that **bacteria** living in deep oceans make their own food, like plants. But these living things do not use the Sun; they use chemicals and heat energy from hot springs on the seabed.

Making food

Green plants make food in their leaves, using a process called **photosynthesis**. The plant takes in carbon dioxide gas from the air through holes in its leaves and takes in water through its roots. During photosynthesis, energy from sunlight is used to convert carbon dioxide and water into a sugar called **glucose**, with oxygen gas as a waste product. The glucose becomes a source of energy that the plant can use.

DID YOU KNOW?

Around half of all photosynthesis on Earth occurs on land, such as in the trees of rain forests. The other half takes place in tiny floating **algae** in oceans.

Plants that catch prey

Some plants, such as the Venus flytrap, are **carnivorous**, which means they eat meat! They carry out photosynthesis to make glucose for energy. However, they live in places such as bogs, where the soil does not contain all the **nutrients** they need. These plants catch and digest insects to obtain these nutrients.

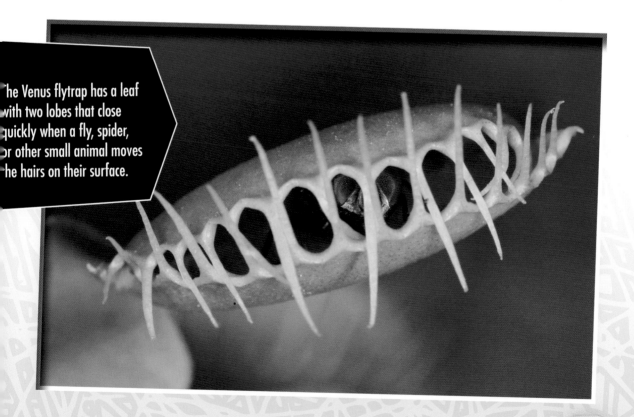

The Venus flytrap has a leaf with two lobes that close quickly when a fly, spider, or other small animal moves the hairs on their surface.

How animals feed

Every animal has special features or **adaptations**, such as particular types of teeth, tongues, or claws, that help them get the food they need. Anteaters eat ants and termites. They lick them up with a long, sticky tongue. Blue whales filter shrimp-like krill from seawater using a fringe of special comb-like teeth. Some animals have special behavior they use to feed. For example, spiders make webs to catch **prey** that they inject with venom. This keeps the prey still while they eat it!

DID YOU KNOW?

Starfish can feed on shells that are closed tightly by forcing them open with their arms. They then push out their stomach through their mouth to digest the animal inside the shell!

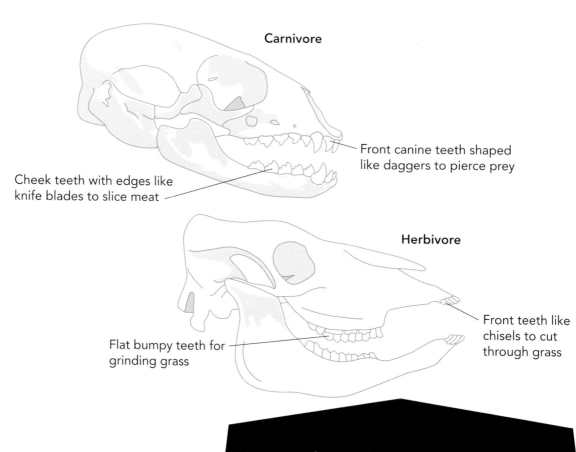

Carnivore

Front canine teeth shaped like daggers to pierce prey

Cheek teeth with edges like knife blades to slice meat

Herbivore

Flat bumpy teeth for grinding grass

Front teeth like chisels to cut through grass

Carnivores such as tigers have long, sharp teeth to kill their prey. They use their jagged back teeth to bite off pieces. Herbivores (plant-eating animals) such as horses have sharp front teeth to bite off grass, and flat back teeth to chew it.

Breaking down food

Digestion is when food is broken down into smaller pieces that a living thing can use. In many animals, teeth, together with saliva, start to digest food. Then, the food moves into the other parts of the **digestive system** called the stomach and intestines. Glands in the digestive system release chemicals that break down different foods. For example, a chemical called hydrochloric acid is made in our stomachs to digest meat.

WHAT'S NEXT?

Scientists can already grow tiny shreds of meat in laboratories. In the future, they may be able to supply large amounts of meat without needing to kill animals.

A chameleon's tongue is as long or longer than its body. It flicks its tongue toward its prey in a fraction of a second. The tongue's tip is covered with sticky spit and has a rough surface to grip the meal.

Transporting food

In many animals, including humans, digested food is moved around the body by the **circulatory system** to wherever energy and nutrients are needed. The circulatory system includes blood, the blood vessels that blood travels through, and the heart that pumps it along. Digested food moves from the intestines into blood vessels, where it is dissolved in blood. The blood containing nutrients moves through the body.

Water is the major part of blood and digestive fluids such as saliva. It is also important in life processes other than nutrition, such as respiration and excretion. In fact, around two-thirds of a human is water! This is why we need to drink plenty of water every day.

Eureka moment!

In 1985, an experienced marathon runner and a scientist developed the first energy gel. It was designed to be a high-energy food that could be digested quickly and fuel the muscles of athletes while they are competing.

Storing food

When living things eat more than they need, they can store the extra energy for times when there is not enough. Plants store glucose as starch in roots, **fruits**, stems, and **seeds**. Animals can store energy as body fat. Some animals, such as brown bears, hibernate, or go into a special form of deep sleep, during the winter. They need to eat lots of food in the weeks before hibernating in order to build up body fat. If people eat too much and do not exercise enough, they can build up so much body fat that they become unhealthy.

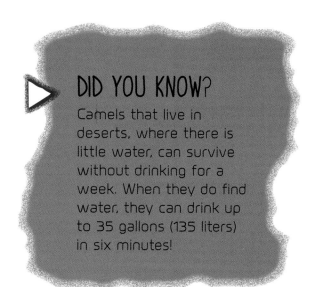

DID YOU KNOW?

Camels that live in deserts, where there is little water, can survive without drinking for a week. When they do find water, they can drink up to 35 gallons (135 liters) in six minutes!

In the fall, brown bears catch and eat as many salmon as possible. These fish are rich in fat. The bears then build up a thick layer of body fat to provide nutrition during the months of inactivity during hibernation.

Try this!

Have you ever drooled when you see or think of a favorite food? Saliva or spit is important in digestion because it contains a substance called amylase. This breaks down starchy foods such as potato and bread into sugars.

Prediction

The amount of starch in foods will decrease when mixed with spit because it will be turned into sugars.

What you need

- Goggles
- Rubber or thin plastic gloves
- Cornstarch
- A teaspoon
- A plate
- A plastic cup
- Iodine with an eyedropper
- Two test tubes or similar thin glass tubes
- A small bowl
- Two plastic or wooden coffee stirrers
- Paper towels
- A stopwatch or clock
- Paper and a pen or pencil

What you do

(1) Put on the goggles and gloves. Place half a teaspoon of cornstarch on the plate and add one drop of iodine. The brown-orange iodine will turn a blue-black color because it reacts with a chemical in starch.

Stay safe!

Wear goggles when using iodine, because it could damage your eyes. It also stains skin, clothes, tabletops, and anything it touches, so wear gloves and carry out the demonstration on newspaper or a rag to protect surfaces. Saliva may contain germs, so don't touch anyone else's.

2 Wash the teaspoon and then use it to measure one teaspoon of water, which you will place in the first tube.

3 Collect saliva from your mouth in the small bowl. Thinking about lemons or a favorite food can help produce more spit! Place one teaspoon of spit in the second tube.

4 Wash and dry the spoon using a paper towel. Put one-third of a teaspoon of cornstarch into each test tube and use a separate stirrer to mix the starch with the liquid.

5 Place the test tubes in a warm place. Stir each test tube every 5 minutes for 20 minutes. Add four drops of iodine to each tube and watch what happens. Record your results.

Conclusion

The color in the tube with water should be darker than the one with spit. This proves that it has more starch in it. That is because amylase in the spit turned the starch to sugars, which do not make the iodine turn black.

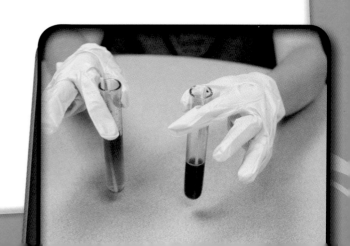

What Is Respiration?

Respiration is the life process that releases energy from glucose. Energy from respiration drives all the other life processes in living things. Respiration usually needs oxygen. Breathing is not the same thing as respiration, but some animals, including people, get oxygen for respiration by breathing it in.

Getting oxygen

Lungs are soft **organs** in our chest that are connected by tubes to our mouth and nostrils. Movements of muscles around the lungs make them get bigger and suck in air. Other animals have different ways of getting oxygen. For example, fish use gills that take oxygen from the water they live in, and frogs can get oxygen from the air through their moist skin. Green plants make oxygen during photosynthesis, but they also take in some air, which contains oxygen, through their leaves. Some even take in air through their bark or special roots that stick out of the ground.

This animal is an axolotl, which lives in dark underground rivers. It gets the oxygen it needs for respiration using red, feathery gills on its neck.

Moving gases

Our circulatory system moves oxygen from air in our lungs to **cells** all around our body. Oxygen dissolves in moist cells that line the lungs. It then moves into blood vessels and attaches to red blood cells. These move with the blood to different parts of the body, transporting oxygen to cells.

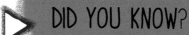

DID YOU KNOW?

Whales have a small blowhole on top of their head to breathe through, rather than their mouth. The blowhole opens when they surface and closes when they dive. This adaptation helps keep water out of their lungs, which would drown them.

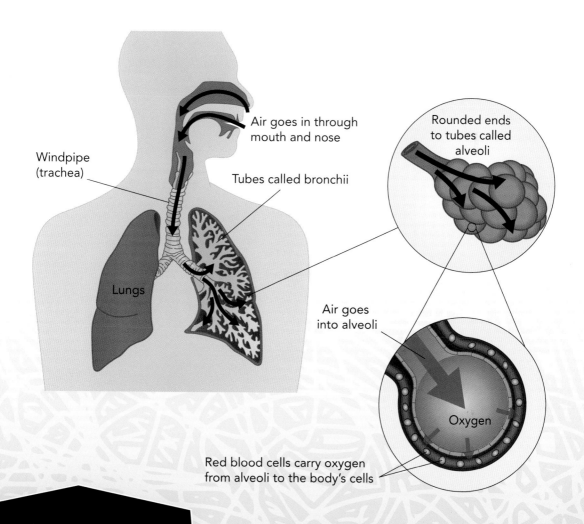

Air goes in through mouth and nose

Windpipe (trachea)

Tubes called bronchii

Lungs

Rounded ends to tubes called alveoli

Air goes into alveoli

Oxygen

Red blood cells carry oxygen from alveoli to the body's cells

This diagram shows how the oxygen moves from air we breathe in into the blood deep inside the lungs.

Try this!

We have a band of muscle called the diaphragm that curves up underneath the lungs. When we breathe in, the diaphragm gets flatter in shape, pulling the base of the lungs down. This action makes the air pressure lower in the lungs than outside the body, which makes the lungs suck in air.

Prediction

Making the pressure lower in a plastic bottle will make it suck in air from outside.

What you need

- Two balloons that can blow up to 10 inches (25 centimeters) across
- A 16-ounce (50-milliliter) plastic bottle
- Duct tape
- A drinking straw
- A pair of scissors

What you do

1. Carefully use the scissors to cut the bottom from the bottle.

2. Without blowing it up, tie off one of the balloons and then cut off its top. Fit the cut end of the tied balloon over the cut bottom of the bottle. You may need to trim the balloon. If you cut off too much, start with a new balloon.

3. Stick the edges of the cut balloon to the bottle with duct tape. Press the tape down to seal the edges. The tied balloon is the diaphragm in your model.

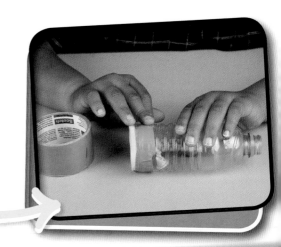

4 Blow up the second balloon two or three times to stretch the rubber, making it easier to inflate later in the demonstration. Push the straw into this balloon and use tape to stick the edges of the balloon neck to the straw. Blow up the balloon through the straw and see if there are any leaks in your tape seal. Then suck on the straw to remove any air trapped inside.

5 Push the second balloon into the bottle through the neck with the straw sticking out of the neck. Use more tape to seal the gap between the straw and the edges of the neck. The balloon in the bottle is the lungs in your model.

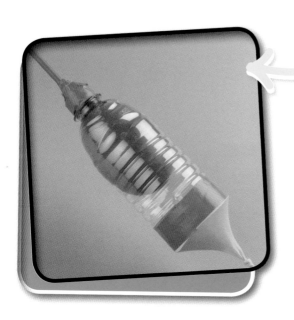

6 Now hold the bottle and pull on the tied balloon end. You should see that the balloon inside the bottle gets bigger. That is because air is sucked in.

Conclusion

Moving the cut balloon outward increases the space for air already in the bottle. This lowers the air pressure, since there is less air in every bit of space. This makes air move in through the bottle neck. The only place it can go is into the balloon, which inflates!

Cells and respiration

All organisms are made of one or more cells. Cells are the tiny building blocks that make up a living thing's body. Each cell carries out essential processes, including respiration. Respiration is the **chemical reaction** between glucose and oxygen to release energy. The glucose and oxygen change into carbon dioxide and water while releasing energy. The respiration reaction happens in special microscopic parts inside cells called mitochondria. Energy released by mitochondria is used by cells to maintain movement, growth, and other processes.

DID YOU KNOW?

Some bacteria can perform respiration without oxygen. This is an adaptation to living in places such as thick mud on seashores, where there is very little oxygen.

Like nearly all other living things, a dolphin is made from cells. It has energy to move and carry out other life processes because of the chemical reactions happening inside the tiny mitochondria inside each cell.

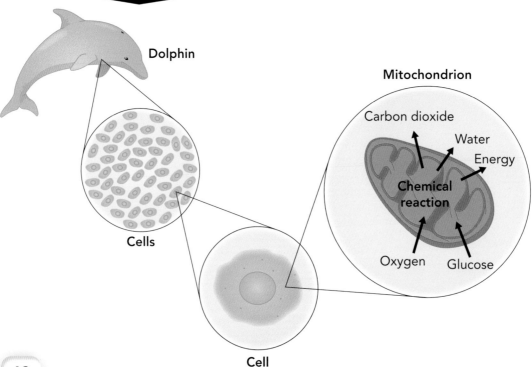

Dolphin

Cells

Cell

Mitochondrion

Carbon dioxide

Water

Energy

Chemical reaction

Oxygen

Glucose

Waste

Cells produce new substances as they carry out different chemical reactions, and one of these is carbon dioxide from respiration. Carbon dioxide can be harmful to cells. Animals and humans get rid of this waste by breathing it out. The carbon dioxide moves from the cells into the blood, which carries it back into the lungs. Other waste products we produce include chemicals in urine (liquid waste) and feces (solid waste). Excretion is the life process that allows living things to get rid of waste that might harm them.

WHAT'S NEXT?

Scientists have found algae living inside salamander **eggs** that supply oxygen to the developing salamanders. The oxygen is a waste product of photosynthesis. One day, scientists may be able to use algae as a source of oxygen for people swimming underwater.

Athletes need their muscle mitochondria to release lots of energy so they can swim, run, or cycle at record speeds. They breathe fast to take in more oxygen to respire glucose in their bodies.

How Do Living Things Grow and Move?

Growth is a life process that allows living things to get bigger, to grow new parts, and also to repair their bodies when injured. Living things grow by increasing the number and size of cells in their body.

More cells

Cells increase in number by dividing in two. First, a cell creates a copy of the parts inside. It then starts to pinch in the middle to become two cells. One cell contains the original cell contents, and the second cell has the copied contents. Finally, the cells split apart.

DID YOU KNOW?

Baby flatfish, such as halibut, hatch from eggs with eyes on either side of their head. Their head grows so that both eyes are on the same side once they start to live on flat seafloors. This allows them to spot danger easily.

Snakes shed all of their outer skin in one piece, revealing a new skin that they have already grown underneath. Worn-out cells rub off people's skin all the time, often becoming part of household dust!

Ways of growing

Different organisms grow in different ways. For example, we humans have bones and muscles that work together to support our bodies and allow us to move. We gradually grow bigger and stronger as we get older. Some other animals grow in short bursts. Insects and crabs have a hard, outer skeleton that is rigid. It means as they grow bigger, their exoskeleton becomes too tight. So, they break out of the old skeleton and grow a new, larger one.

WHAT'S NEXT?

Scientists have discovered that the jaws of rag worms are tougher than human teeth. In the future, a material like this might be grown in labs and used to construct spaceships!

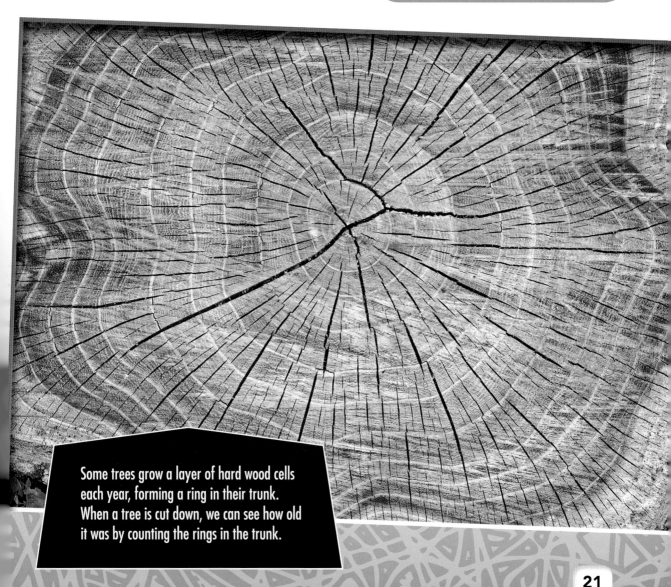

Some trees grow a layer of hard wood cells each year, forming a ring in their trunk. When a tree is cut down, we can see how old it was by counting the rings in the trunk.

Moving plants

Movement is another life process that is different in all organisms. Plants cannot move from place to place like animals, but they do move on the spot, and they usually move slowly. For example, flowers on mountains may close up their petals to protect the delicate inner parts from damage by frost during cold nights. Some plants can move fast. Venus flytraps close shut in an instant to trap flies.

Young sunflowers can turn during the day to face the Sun as it moves across the sky. The heat can help the plant's seeds to develop.

Ways of moving

We blow up an air mattress to make it firm enough to sleep on by pumping in air. In a similar way, plants move by filling their cells with water. Once each cell is full, the water pushes on its outer wall. With all the cells working together, this can make the plant rigid and less likely to bend over. Climbing plants, such as scarlet runner beans, move by growing up other plants or specially placed sticks. Then the beans are not shaded from sunlight by other plants.

tendril grows around another plant

Beans and peas move up toward the light using curly parts, called tendrils, that grow around sticks and branches when they touch them.

Eureka moment!

In 1880, Charles Darwin and his son Francis discovered that the tip of a grass seedling is sensitive to light, but it is the part below the tip that bends it toward the light. When light hits the tip, it causes a chemical to be made that moves into and builds up in cells on the darker side. This makes them grow bigger and bend the tip over toward the light.

Try this!

Demonstrate the light-seeking abilities of plants by setting a bean plant a challenge.

Prediction

A bean plant will grow the shortest distance through a maze to move toward the light.

Note: You can buy scarlet runner bean plants in garden centers in late spring. You could also plant a bean seed in a pot full of moistened compost and keep it in a warm, dark place for several days until a shoot emerges. Then put it in a light place, keeping the soil moist, for about a week, until the plant has two large leaves.

What you need:

- A small, potted scarlet runner bean plant
- A cardboard box; extra cardboard
- A utility knife (to be used by an adult only)
- Scissors
- Duct tape
- A flashlight
- Pencil or pen

Hole cut in top of box

What you do

1 Ask an adult to cut a hole about 1 inch (2.5 centimeters) square in the top of the box to let in light. Use the extra cardboard to construct four sections inside the box.

2 Place the plant in the bottom of the box and use tape to secure it. Now create a maze of sunlight by cutting holes in the other dividers. Decide upon a path and mark the openings with the pen. Remove each inner divider, cut a 1-inch (2.5-centimeter) hole in it, and replace it in the box.

3 Seal the box closed with tape. Put the box in a dark place and shine the flashlight into the top hole. If you can see any light escaping, tape up the gaps.

4 Put the box on a windowsill or table next to a sunny window for three days. Open the box to water the plant. Note what is happening to the plant. Then seal the box again as in step 3.

5 Repeat step 4 until the plant emerges from the top hole. This usually takes about two weeks. Open the box fully and see what route the plant took.

Conclusion

The bean plant grows through the holes you cut. This is because the plant senses sunlight entering the box. It will usually grow the shortest route through the maze toward the light, in order to use as little energy as possible for growth.

Moving animals

Kangaroos hop, birds flap their wings, and snakes slither to move along. Animals move in very different ways, but many use muscles to move parts of their skeleton. A muscle can usually pull in one direction only, so movements may require several muscles. For example, humans bend an arm using the biceps muscle and straighten it using the triceps. Movement of rows of muscles along a snake's body allow its skin to grip the ground and push itself along.

WHAT'S NEXT?

Geckos grip onto smooth surfaces using microscopic hairs on the bottom of their feet. Scientists are copying this hairy skin to make new materials that grip. Their uses include the feet of climbing robots and surgical dressings that hold wounds together without stitches.

Gibbons live high in rain forests. They have long arms to swing between trees, and hands with long, curved fingers to grasp branches.

Adaptations for movement

Animals have many special features that allow them to move using as little energy as possible, so that there is more to use for other life processes. For example, cheetahs have very flexible backbones to stretch their legs far apart to get a long stride. They have sharp claws that they use like running shoe spikes to grip the ground.

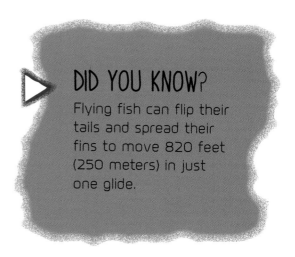

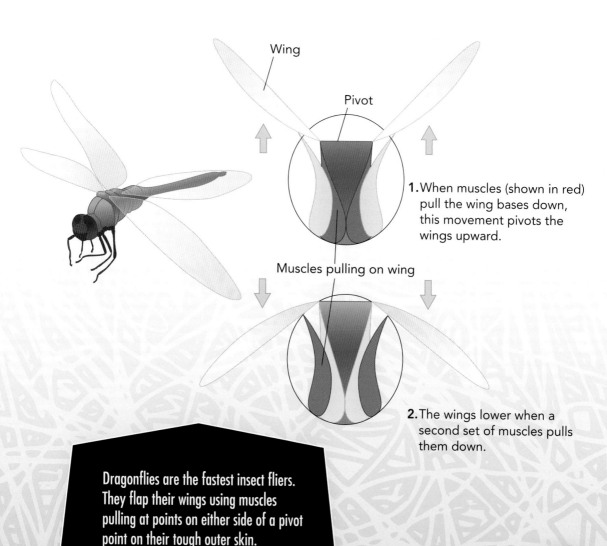

Wing

Pivot

1. When muscles (shown in red) pull the wing bases down, this movement pivots the wings upward.

Muscles pulling on wing

2. The wings lower when a second set of muscles pulls them down.

Dragonflies are the fastest insect fliers. They flap their wings using muscles pulling at points on either side of a pivot point on their tough outer skin.

What Is Sensitivity?

Sensitivity is the ability of an organism to react and respond to changes in the environment. A change that can be detected is called a **stimulus**. For example, the stimulus of seeing an approaching fox or owl would make a rabbit run for its life.

DID YOU KNOW?

Unripe fruit can be made to ripen in a bag containing other ripe fruit. The unripe fruit sense a ripening chemical released by the ripe fruit. This is why whole orchards of fruit trees have ripe fruit at the same time.

Star-nosed moles have amazing noses. The rays of the star are always moving. The moles use them to touch and sense the world around them as they move through the darkness of underground tunnels.

Plant sensitivity

Most plants are rooted in the ground, but it is just as important that they respond to environmental stimuli. For example, a plant's root tips must grow down into the soil to anchor the plant and reach water and nutrients. The root tips know which way is down because of their sensitivity to gravity. Gravity is the force pulling objects toward the center of Earth. Some plants are sensitive to touch. Mimosa leaves fold up when they are touched. Scientists think this sudden movement is an adaptation to scare off leaf-eating insects.

Eureka moment!

In 2007, American scientists discovered that cowpea plants can recognize chemicals made by caterpillars that are eating and digesting their leaves. This makes them produce their own chemicals that attract wasps, which then eat or lay their eggs in the caterpillars!

Falling temperatures and drought conditions in the fall stimulate the leaves of some trees to change color and fall off. This stops the tree from being damaged by wind and snow in the winter.

What are the sense organs?

Sense organs are special structures that we use to detect a stimulus. Eyes are sensitive to light, and ears are sensitive to movements of air that make sounds. The tongue and inside of the nose are sensitive to different chemicals in food or air.

All of these sense organs are on the head, but others are spread around the body. Special cells in our skin detect changes in pressure and temperature. Messages about the different stimuli from sense organs move through nerves to the brain. This processes the messages and tells the body how to move or react.

Eureka moment!

In 2012, two blind men were fitted with light-sensitive electronic pads behind their retina. The pads sent electrical messages into their optic nerve when stimulated by light. They allowed the men to see for the first time in years!

People who are blind can learn to read using Braille. Letters making up words are formed from a pattern or code of raised bumps that the readers can feel with their fingertips.

How eyes work

In the eyes of most animals, a transparent lens directs light onto light-sensitive cells. These create an electrical message in response to the light stimulus, which travels to the brain. In humans, the cells detecting changes in light strength and color are collected together in a structure called the retina. The amount of light reaching the retina is controlled by the iris, which opens and closes depending on how bright it is.

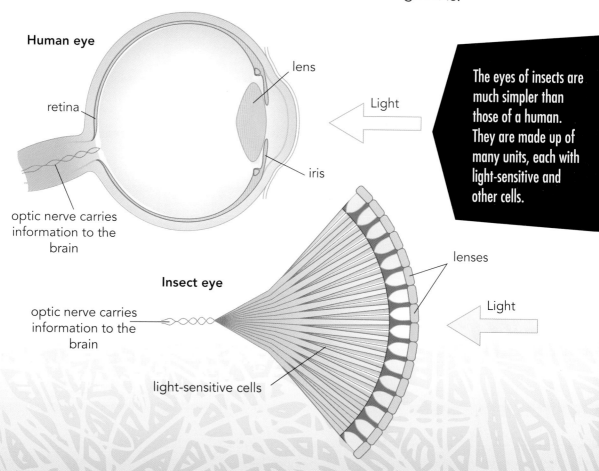

Human eye

retina

lens

Light

iris

optic nerve carries information to the brain

The eyes of insects are much simpler than those of a human. They are made up of many units, each with light-sensitive and other cells.

lenses

Light

Insect eye

optic nerve carries information to the brain

light-sensitive cells

DID YOU KNOW?

Insects can see around 100 times less detail than humans because they have far fewer light-sensitive cells. They can detect shape and brightness but cannot distinguish the depth and position of things around them. However, insects can detect movement about six times better than we can, because their eye cells are more sensitive to slight changes in light intensity than ours. That is why flies move so quickly when people try to swat them!

Using senses

Many animals have the same five senses as humans. However, their sense organs are in different places. For example, the taste receptors of octopuses are on their arms. The importance of each sense depends on what the animal needs to do in its life to survive. For example, cats are nighttime predators. They have many sensitive whiskers on their face that help them find their way around. A shiny layer behind cats' retinas reflects light back onto the retina, so that they can see better in the dark.

Many animals that are nocturnal (active at night) have large eyes and sometimes large ears to hear movements of other animals.

Other senses

Some animals are sensitive to things that humans cannot detect. For example, female mosquitoes can detect the amount of carbon dioxide in the air. This sensitivity helps them find **mammals** breathing out the gas. They then bite the mammals to drink their blood! Some animals, such as sea turtles, are thought to detect Earth's magnetic field, which is a network of magnetic forces around the planet. Turtles probably use this sense to find their way across oceans to feeding and breeding places.

DID YOU KNOW?

Vipers are snakes that can detect heat changes of as little as two-thousandths of a degree. This is an adaptation for finding warm-blooded mammal prey, such as mice, in the dark.

A hammerhead shark uses sense organs on the underside of its wide head to detect the weak electricity produced by muscles in prey such as flatfish or rays buried under mud.

Eureka moment!

In 2012, scientists discovered tiny pieces of a magnetic substance called magnetite in cells in the noses of rainbow trout. These help the fish navigate by twisting in Earth's magnetic field, like the needle on a compass!

How Do Living Things Reproduce?

Every living thing is a member of a **species**, or type of organism. All individuals eventually die, and the species would eventually disappear if there were not any other individuals to take their place. Reproduction is the life process allowing every species to make new organisms similar to themselves.

Reproduction for one

One of the two main methods of reproduction is called **asexual reproduction**. Young that are produced asexually come from a single parent. For example, an onion plant grows from a **bulb** and can produce several identical small bulbs from its sides. Animals such as aphids and sea anemones can also reproduce asexually. The young organism is identical to its parent because its cells are exact copies.

DID YOU KNOW?

The egg-laying queen driver ant can lay 3 to 4 million eggs each month. Most hatch into nearly identical worker ants that cannot reproduce. The ants live together in groups of up to 20 million.

A sea anemone's identical offspring grow from its base by asexual reproduction. They break off and are washed away by moving seawater until they attach themselves to rocks and grow bigger.

Two parents

Many species produce young by sexual reproduction. Male and female individuals each produce **sex cells**, which are special cells grown for reproduction. The male and female sex cells join in the process of **fertilization**. The young produced through fertilization combine characteristics of each parent passed on in the sex cells. Some living things, such as plants, have both male and female parts for producing sex cells.

Eureka moment!

In 2001, a baby hammerhead shark was born in a U.S. aquarium. Sharks normally reproduce sexually, but this shark's mother had never come into contact with male sharks. Scientists discovered that the baby was identical to its mother and was produced by asexual reproduction.

Kittens are produced by sexual reproduction and are slightly different than their parents.

Bats are attracted to the strong smell of sweet nectar from cactus flowers. As they lap up the liquid, flower pollen rubs onto their fur. The bats carry this pollen to the next flowers they feed on.

Flowering plants

The most colorful plants grow flowers to reproduce with. They often have a central female part called a carpel, which makes parts called ovules containing sex cells. Around the carpel, there are male parts called stamens. Stamens produce grains called pollen that contain different sex cells. A plant can fertilize another plant when its pollen reaches the other's carpel. This movement is called pollination.

Plants pollinate in many different ways. Some attract animals using scent and colored petals and by supplying a sweet liquid called nectar. When animals visit a flower to drink the nectar, they pick up or drop off pollen from other flowers. Other plants, such as grasses, use wind to blow their pollen. Once pollination has happened, the male sex cells move from the pollen. They fertilize the female sex cells in the ovules. These form seeds.

 DID YOU KNOW?

A plant called the titan arum produces a reproductive part 9 feet (3 meters) high with lots of flowers on it. The flowers make a smell similar to a dead body, to attract flies as pollinators!

Seeds

A seed contains a young plant and its supply of food. The seeds of plants such as apples develop inside fruits that are often fleshy and sweet. This attracts animals to eat the fruit. When the animals produce droppings, they spread the seeds in other places where the plant might grow. Other plants protect their seeds in tough structures, to prevent animals from eating them. For example, chestnut and hazel trees make their seeds in hard, tough nuts.

Some trees, including pine and spruce, are conifers. They make their papery seeds between the overlapping scales in protective woody cones.

Eureka moment!

In 2012, scientists grew plants from seeds around 30,000 years old. The seeds had survived in frozen soil, where they had been stored as a food supply by squirrels!

Sexual reproduction in animals

In many animals, including insects and people, male sex cells are called sperm, and female sex cells are eggs. In many living things, the male puts the sperm inside the female. Most animals then lay the fertilized eggs and leave the young to hatch and care for themselves. Female fish and frogs usually lay their eggs in water. The male then sprays sperm on top of the eggs.

DID YOU KNOW?

Fertilized eggs of one type of Surinam toad from South America stick to and sink into the female's skin. The skin grows over them, and the tadpoles that hatch from each egg develop safely on her back. They eventually break out as tiny, fully developed toads!

Birds lay eggs with tough shells that protect the chicks before they are developed enough to hatch. Some chicks can then care for themselves, but many are helpless and rely on their parents for protection and to bring them food.

Giving birth

Fertilized mammal eggs develop inside their mother, and then she gives birth to her babies. Some baby mammals, such as giraffes, are well developed at birth and can even walk around. Others, such as human babies, are too weak to survive on their own. Adult female mammals can produce milk rich in nutrients and energy that they feed to their babies, to help them develop.

Eureka moment!

In 1978, the first human test-tube baby was born. A test-tube baby is fertilized in a laboratory using eggs and sperm collected from parents who cannot have a baby naturally.

Baby kangaroos are tiny and helpless when first born. They crawl inside a flap of skin on the mother's stomach, called a pouch, where they feed and grow in safety.

Successful reproduction

Giving birth or laying eggs creates a new individual, but reproduction is not successful unless the baby survives. Many animals, such as humans, cats, and orcas, use lots of energy and time keeping their young safe and well fed and teaching them how to survive. Some animals reproduce and raise many young over many years. For others, reproduction is the end of their life. Male honeybees die as soon as they have mated. Male spiders of some species are eaten by the female they have mated with and become a source of nutrition for her eggs!

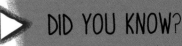

DID YOU KNOW?

Babies of amphibians called caecilians eat their mother's skin when she sheds it. The skin contains nutrients to help them grow.

Each year, millions of red crabs move from where they live on land—in forests on Christmas Island, Australia—to the seashore, where they mate. Females lay their fertilized eggs in the sea. The eggs hatch and develop into crabs, which then move back to the island to live.

Life cycles

A life cycle includes all the life stages from birth to death. Some organisms have life cycles with many different stages. For example, butterflies hatch from eggs as caterpillars that feed and grow, before changing into pupas. An adult butterfly emerges from the pupa. Life cycles vary greatly in length, from 7 days for a mosquito to over 40 years for some beetles.

eggs

tadpole

adult frog

tadpole with legs

young frog

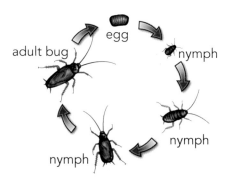

adult bug

egg

nymph

nymph

nymph

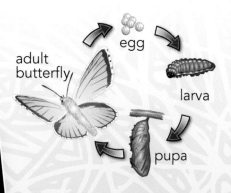

adult butterfly

egg

larva

pupa

Every type of living thing has a typical life cycle. The young of frogs and butterflies (tadpoles or larvae) look totally different than the adults. However, the nymphs that hatch from the eggs of bugs look like smaller versions of the adults.

Challenges to Life Processes

Living things in the wild face many challenges, many of which are caused by humans. For example, people cut down forests to get wood and to make new farmland. This means a loss of **habitat** and food for the animals that live in the forests.

Another problem is pollution, which happens when dirty, harmful, or dangerous substances are added to air, water, or soil—usually by people. For example, nutrients in fertilizer (used for making crops grow better) wash from farmland into rivers. They then become food for river algae, which grow so fast they use up all the oxygen in the water. Then river fish die because they cannot perform respiration. When there are fewer fish to eat, river birds may not have enough to eat.

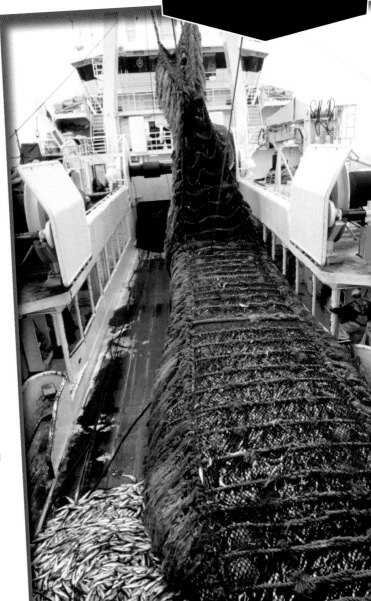

When people catch too many fish, there are fewer young fish to grow into adults that can reproduce. In some parts of the ocean, fish that were once common, such as cod, are now rare because of overfishing.

▷ DID YOU KNOW?

Air pollution causes respiration difficulties for many people and kills over one million people each year.

Helping life processes

People can help the life processes of other organisms in different ways. For example, they can preserve habitats where the organisms live. They can keep and protect **endangered** animals in reserves and zoos. People can sometimes encourage animals to reproduce by finding males for females to mate with.

This is a baby giant panda. Pandas are slow to reproduce naturally, and many cubs are abandoned by their mothers and die. People can help these rare animals to reproduce more successfully by hand-raising abandoned cubs until they are able to care for themselves.

Eureka moment!

In 2009, Spanish scientists announced that a mountain goat had been born. But this kind of goat was extinct, meaning it had died out. The scientists had transferred parts of cells from the skin of a dead goat into the fertilized egg of an ordinary goat.

Glossary

adaptation physical feature or behavior that helps a living thing survive in a particular environment

algae simple living things that make food in the same way as plants but have no leaves, stems, or roots

asexual reproduction reproduction by making identical copies of an individual rather than by combining sex cells

bacteria tiny living things found everywhere. Some bacteria cause diseases, while others break down waste.

bulb rounded underground part of plants such as onions or daffodils. The plant grows from the bulb each year.

carnivorous when an animal or plant eats meat

cell smallest unit of a living thing that can exist on its own, carrying out a range of life processes. Most organisms are made of many cells.

chemical reaction when two or more substances mix and rearrange to become different substances

circulatory system set of organs for moving blood and transporting substances such as oxygen and glucose around an organism's body

digestive system organs and body parts that work together to process and digest food

egg female sex cell of an animal, which can be fertilized by sperm

endangered when a type of organism is at risk of dying out

environment conditions such as weather, plants, type of soil, and animals where an organism lives

excretion process of getting rid of waste substances produced by life processes

fertilization when a male sex cell joins with a female sex cell to make a new living thing

fruit part of a plant where seeds develop

glucose type of sugar that is the source of energy in living things

habitat place where an animal or plant naturally lives because the area provides the things needed to carry out its life processes

mammal warm-blooded animal that usually has fur or hair and drinks milk from its mother when it is young

nutrient chemical necessary for the healthy growth and functioning of living things

nutrition ability to take in or make food as a source of energy and chemicals that are important for health

organ part of the body with a particular function, such as the heart or stomach

parasite living thing that lives in or on another, usually causing it harm

photosynthesis process in green plants that uses the Sun's energy to make glucose from carbon dioxide and water

prey animal that is caught and eaten by another animal

reproduction ability to produce offspring or young

respiration process in living things that releases energy from food

seed tough part made by plants containing a fertilized ovule that a new plant can grow from

sex cell type of cell produced for sexual reproduction

species type of organism different from all other types, such as a human or an ostrich. A member of one species can only reproduce sexually with another member of the same species.

stimulus something that produces a reaction in a living thing, such as a loud sound

Find Out More

Books

Claybourne, Anna. *Life Processes* (Web of Life). Chicago: Raintree, 2012.

Guillain, Charlotte. *Life Cycles* (Investigate!). Chicago: Heinemann Library, 2008.

Snedden, Robert. *Adaptation and Survival* (Web of Life). Chicago: Raintree, 2012.

Somervill, Barbara. *Animal Cells and Life Processes* (Investigating Cells). Chicago: Heinemann Library, 2011.

Web sites

www.kidsbiology.com/biology_basics/needs_living_things/living_things_have_needs1.php

Learn more about living things and their needs at this web site.

pbskids.org/dragonflytv/show/livingthings.html

This web site features fun videos about all kinds of living things.

Places to visit

Exploratorium
Pier 15
San Francisco, California 94111

www.exploratorium.edu

This museum examines many different aspects of science and offers hands-on activities. Visit the "Traits of Life" exhibit to learn more about living things.

The Health Museum
1515 Hermann Drive
Houston, Texas 77004

www.mhms.org

Discover more about you and your body in interactive exhibits at this museum.

Further research

- A mosquito's life cycle is seven days long, but some wood-boring beetles have a 40-year life cycle. Research the different lengths of life cycles in living things. Why do you think they are so different?

- Some athletes train at high altitude, where the air pressure is lower than nearer sea level. Find out how this affects their respiration and allows them to run for longer.

- In deserts, living things can struggle to get the food and water they need and to move across the shifting sands. Find out about adaptations that camels, snakes, and other living things use to maintain their life processes in this challenging environment. You could look at adaptations for life in other environments, too, such as Antarctica or the oceans.

Index